WHY WE GATHER

I don't know about you, but I get giddy with excitement when it comes to planning a gathering. Actually, I get giddy with excitement when it comes to planning pretty much anything. In this digital-dependent world, it is satisfying to put pen to paper and write out the details that go into creating an event. And seeing the pure joy of those I have invited to gather is worth every second of that fun dreaming and planning and list-making.

Taking the time to plan a gathering allows you to set an intention before you set the table, to choose a mood before you choose a menu. Then you can focus on the details you want to include. It's no fun hosting a special occasion, only to find out you forgot the sparkler candles for the cake. I've been there, my friend. Let's not let a few mishaps spoil the wonder of bringing people around a table and sharing life together.

I created this planner so you'll never miss out on the gift of gathering. I want you to build your mental pantry of ideas, recipes, and tips as you build excitement and confidence for your next celebration, party, or casual get-together. This helpful guide is designed to make your next event a success. (And a good measure of success, in my opinion, is that you have as much fun as your guests do.) Grab your favorite beverage and take a moment to sit and write out the who, what, where, and why of the gathering you are planning. Allow yourself a moment to daydream about how the gathering will look, feel, sound, and delight. Jot down any details that come to mind so you can be sure to include them. You'll never run out of ideas for special touches when you draw inspiration from nature and the seasons, the people who are on your guest list, a special recipe you can't wait to try, or the many gifts you'd like to give those who gather.

When all the planning, preparation, setup, and addition of special details for your guests unfold in a unique get-together, there is always a moment you'll tuck away in your heart. Whether it's big or small, this moment, this special scene, captures the sentiment of the gathering—the smile of a guest, the twinkling lights illuminating everyone's faces, the oohs and aahs when the dessert is placed in the center of the table, the sound of kids laughing and playing at the barbecue. Pause for a moment to soak it all in. Cherish it. Savor the details, and then come back and write them down so you'll always remember...

This is why.

This is why we plan, why we prepare.

This is why we gather.

JOYFUL PLANS

I should first let you know that I'm a habitual procrastinator. I learned the hard way that planning is my friend and not a mean taskmaster. Planning will be your friend too. When the stress kicks in and we're fretting over a missing plate or hollering orders to our family in a moment of frustration, we can refocus on why we're doing this and who we're doing it for. It makes all the difference and allows for the joy of the gathering to nudge us through procrastination or when we have that "What have I gotten myself into?" moment.

Start with the information included on most event invitations. This is your research stage of planning. Determine your reason to gather, choose who you will invite, and then decide when and where. Is it a "just because" get-together? A holiday celebration, birthday, or life event? This information helps you brainstorm and become excited to make plans.

It's not about us. Sure, we're incorporating elements we love, but ultimately we're creating a welcoming space for our guests. When we lose sight of that, we put unnecessary pressure on ourselves and turn into unhappy, harried hosts who don't help people to feel welcome. I've been that person. And then I learned to give myself plenty of time to get ready, plan, and prepare for my gathering.

I'll never forget the very first time I was ready before our guests arrived. I kept checking the front window to see if anyone was approaching and then running back to my table to see if I had forgotten anything. Finally, my husband told me to sit and wait for our company to come. After a few minutes, I let out a deep sigh of relief and said, "So this is what being ready on time feels like?" We laughed because we both remembered when I would run around the house desperately rounding up items for the place settings, wiping smudges off plates with a towel, tidying up (shoving miscellaneous items into drawers)...all because I didn't prepare ahead of time.

I hadn't appreciated the joyful benefits of planning until that day. I was a convert the moment I opened the door to the first guests, welcomed them with a sense of peace, and gave them my full attention instead of worrying about last-minute details. Being present to our guests is one of the greatest presents we can give them.

Setting the Tone

Once you know who you're inviting and when and where you'll gather, you can start imagining and planning the look and feel of your occasion. Create the tone for the event by considering three pieces of the planning puzzle—mood, inspiration, and color.

MOOD

We can evoke the mood we want by setting the scene. Every basic element has a purpose, and every special touch adds to the ambiance and overall experience. Coming up with just a word or two might be enough to get your wheels turning. Don't overthink this. Just ask yourself how you want the gathering to feel. What mood would you love to evoke in your guests? Here are some words to help you get started...

LIGHT	CHILDLIKE	REFLECTIVE	WHIMSICAL
CASUAL	HAPPY	ROMANTIC	LAID-BACK
LIVELY	COZY	GROWN-UP	CELEBRATORY
SERENE	LOW-KEY	FORMAL	FESTIVE
JOYFUL	INTIMATE	FUN/PLAYFUL	ELEGANT

I use the term "mood" a bit loosely. It's the vibe your gathering will inspire. Asking myself about the mood I want to create often gives me focus and leads me to the best ideas.

INSPIRATION

My ideas start blooming at this point because I know who is coming and why we're gathering. I know the mood I want to evoke. Now I choose an inspiration for this get-together to help me stay on track. It can be easy to get carried away with too many additions or to get stuck trying to decide exactly what to add. Defining a theme or an inspirational concept will help. A list of some key elements you want to incorporate can help you remember the look and feel you are going for.

Maybe you're inspired by an artistic era, like the art deco of the '20s, or a home style, such as country cottage. Inspiration for a gathering might come from a trip you took to Italy or a dinner you had at a chic restaurant. Did an online or magazine photo stick with you? Maybe the view from your porch is all the inspiration you need. I love movies, so I will often imagine a scene I want to emulate in my tablescape's style, presentation, and colors. Sources of inspiration are endless.

COLOR

Motivated by the mood and inspiration, I then begin to dream in color. Often, I take cues from nature because every season of the year presents its own shades of beauty. Discovering decor ideas in God's creation is a great idea. In fact, you and I might be compelled to send out those invites simply to celebrate the show creation is putting on!

It simplifies planning so much to choose colors to suit the mood you're going for and the spirit of the season. For example, in spring, I choose light and cool tones. In the fall, I want warm, rich colors. My best advice is to choose and stick with three colors for a pleasing and cohesive table decor. You could use one color in three different shades, or you could incorporate three different colors throughout the table.

For example, when I use fresh flowers, I like to coordinate the main flowers with other colors on the table, whether they are in the dishes or the napkins. Using only three colors keeps things from looking too busy and will help you decide which plates, glasses, and other items to use.

Just as I enjoy picturing loved ones around a beautiful table, I love to visualize what needs to occur in advance so the anticipated gathering happens with ease. This serves me well, and I want to help you do the same. The following at-a-glance timeline prompts you to think through essential details and discover a planning pace that suits your style.

Simple Planning Timeline

THREE DAYS BEFORE

- Plan your meal.

- Do any deep cleaning that needs to be done.

- Purchase any pieces you might be wishing to incorporate on your table, such as new table linens or stemware.

TWO DAYS BEFORE

- Pull out the items you intend to use on your table. Plates, silverware, candlesticks, other tablescape elements. This is particularly important for any items you don't use daily.

ONE DAY BEFORE

- For a formal or more elaborate gathering, if you can, set the table in advance. By not waiting until the day of the gathering, you will have more time to focus on the food and any last-minute cleaning.

- Prepare any food that can be made the day before.

DAY OF

- Get any food prep out of the way first thing in the morning. That way when you begin to cook, you're not losing time dicing vegetables or slicing cheese.

TWO HOURS BEFORE

- Make sure you're ready! There's nothing like being caught still in your sweats.

- Begin cooking. I try to time foods so they are done about 20 minutes after guests have arrived. This gives me time to catch up with guests and pour drinks.

TWENTY MINUTES BEFORE

- Light candles and turn on some music to create an atmosphere that contributes to the overall feel of getting together.

- Relax. Say a prayer. Think about the gift of gathering.

TABLESCAPE BASICS

tablescape (noun): *an artistic arrangement of articles on a table*

Your table is your foundation. Whether it's a picnic table, a card table in an apple orchard, a breakfast bar, or a farmhouse table like mine, it's the blank canvas that is ready for your creative touches to make every gathering unique. No two gatherings are the same; however, we will use basic elements to prepare any table for guests to gather together.

Tablescape Elements

Creating tablescapes is much more than just having a grand design. It's about combining fun little details that welcome our guests to a memorable experience. We'll look at the three primary elements—linens, centerpieces, and place settings—and then consider some special touches that can add to the occasion.

LINENS

Linens hold a special place in my heart. Soon after my husband and I got married, my mother gifted me my first set of cloth napkins. I imagine I gave her a slightly bewildered look. However, it didn't take me too long to discover how using cloth napkins (instead of paper) made our dining experience seem more special. They were the added touch that made everyday meals feel a bit more meaningful and substantial.

I like real linen. It has an elegant feel, but the natural look of the fabric keeps things relaxed. If I want my table to feel more dressed up, I add a tablecloth, and if I want to create extra layers, I might place another tablecloth on top or include a plush table runner.

CENTERPIECES

Creating a centerpiece is a great way to add interest to your table. I approach this a few different ways. If I create a centerpiece that can't easily be moved, then I make sure to set up a serving station where guests can fill their plates. You could also strategically place a centerpiece in a tray so it can easily be removed from the table to make room for food when it's time to eat.

The centerpiece provides a significant way to share your personal style and set the mood of the gathering. You can use candles, an artful display of a seasonal element, or your favorite flowers from the grocery store. If you need more ideas, I have the book for you! In *The Gift of Gathering,* I offer a dozen of my favorite gatherings with a unique centerpiece for each. I include suggestions and inspiration that can serve as a springboard for your own ideas. But for now, here are some simple tips on flower arranging.

My 12 Favorite Vessels for Flower Arranging

farmhouse pitcher

amber bottles

juice carafe

galvanized metal bucket

old canning jars

footed urns

creamers

antique silver pitcher

pedestal vase

grouping of cylinder vases

wooden crate

terra-cotta jug

Tip: *Using food as part of your centerpiece is also a great way to make your table come alive. Think fresh fruit in the summer or spring—oranges, grapefruit, figs, peaches, lemons, and limes. Try harvest vegetables for the fall or winter months—apples, butternut squash, acorn squash, pumpkins, gourds, pears, artichokes, or flowering kale (my personal favorite).*

DIY Pedestal Vase and Floral Arrangement

ITEMS YOU'LL NEED

2 salad bowls

Superglue

1 block of floral foam

3 kinds of florals of different sizes
(try combining roses, Hypericum berries, and white scabiosa)

Greenery
(I love variegated pittosporum)

INSTRUCTIONS

1. Two salad bowls glued together make the perfect pedestal vessel. Flip one over and stack the other on top. Use Gorilla Glue or a superglue to attach the two bowls.

2. Cut the block of floral foam into thirds. Place them in the vessel.

3. Circle the base of the arrangement along the bowl with about 10 of the largest flowers.

4. Once the bottom circle is complete, stagger about 6 more flowers to create a second row or "inner circle" on top.

5. Next, take the second floral and fill in around and in between the large flowers.

6. Now use greenery to fill in any remaining gaps in the arrangement.

7. Finally, add smaller pops of color with your last (and smallest) flower.

Tip: *When picking flowers, choose something that is in season and complements a color from your dishes or linens.*

Five Flower Arrangement Ideas

USE ONE KIND OF FLOWER

Fill a large galvanized metal bucket with all of the same type of flower. Hydrangeas are great because they fill a lot of space. Other great varieties include tulips, lilacs, peonies, roses, or just greens (seeded eucalyptus is my personal favorite!).

USE ONE COLOR

I like to make this type of arrangement when I'm wanting a more professional-looking arrangement. I pick three kinds of flowers in the same color (white tulips, white ranunculus, and white peonies, for example). Since all flower stems are green, I sometimes pop in a few greens to help fill out my arrangement and keep my costs lower. Or you can leave the filler greens out for a crisper, tighter arrangement with just the flowers.

MY GO-TO FLOWER ARRANGEMENT

Without fail, I grab the same three kinds of flowers from Trader Joe's when I want to make a quick, beautiful flower arrangement. This is my first choice anytime I want to add flowers to my dining table or coffee table—or to have them just because. They are white hydrangeas, eucalyptus (seeded or silver dollar), and dusty miller (a silver, frosted looking leaf).

My Tablescape Inventory

Tips for Arranging the Food Table

Setting up a side table or buffet to arrange food on can be as fun and exciting as creating a tablescape for your gathering. I believe the key to a successful food table is the presentation of the food. One of my go-to ideas for arranging food on a buffet is to grab my cake stands. I love displaying them in my kitchen on our open shelves as pretty decor, and they are easy to grab at a moment's notice when I'm arranging food. Here are five tips you can use to arrange a food table for any gathering.

ADD HEIGHT

Do you sometimes run out of room on your food table? You might not be able to add more horizontal surface, but using cake stands or crates flipped upside down to style food is a great way not only to add height to your display but also to create more serving space. I love to stack smaller cake stands on top of larger ones to add even more height. Whether you are using a small table, a kitchen island, or a dining room buffet (like I do), adding height gives you more room to style and display your food.

INCORPORATE VARYING SIZES

Along with adding height, I like to use various sizes of serving platters. This helps each dish or food item you are serving stand out and become even more noticeable. Incorporating different sizes adds interest and keeps your eyes moving throughout the display.

SET UP A DRINK STATION

Designating a drink station makes hosting any event easier. Picture this...as guests arrive, you greet each person, welcome them in, take their jacket, and ask what they would like to drink. You can imagine how much running around that entails as you do this for each guest, especially if they arrive back to back. Setting up a drink station allows you to welcome each guest and invite them to fill a glass with a beverage of their choice.

To prepare ahead of time, I fill up a pitcher with water and set some lemon wedges in a ramekin nearby. I also set out a decanter with a specialty drink (this can be alcoholic or nonalcoholic) and a large metal tub filled with ice and bottled choices. This is extremely handy when you are hosting lots of guests with kids. My tub includes a few different juice box options and some fun flavored water to keep kiddos happy. They can grab a new drink whenever they need one, which helps Mom and Dad relax!

Tip: When using a decanter with a spout, be sure to place it on top of a cake stand or small wooden crate turned upside down. That will provide room to fill glasses underneath the spout.

USE ALL WHITE SERVEWARE

Whenever I am styling a buffet to serve food on, I grab all my white plates and bowls. This makes the food look more appetizing, and it also allows me to mix and match my pieces or easily add to a set if something breaks. Keeping things in the same color also creates a more cohesive look on your food table and a more upscale display.

DON'T FORGET THE DETAILS

I always say it's the details that really make something memorable. Set out some cute paper straws or toothpicks with tiny washi-tape flags attached to one end. Wrap your silverware and napkin together with striped baker's twine or pretty ribbon. Your guests will notice and appreciate these tiny details—even if you're using plastic utensils!

After all your hard work, don't forget to sit back, relax, and enjoy your company. As much as I love to prepare, plan, and host, I'm most excited about spending quality time with people in my life.

PLANNING PAGES

As hosts, we are extra lucky. We get to savor the memories of preparing for guests and of enjoying their company. That's why I wanted to create this planner. It will become your blessing book! These unique planning pages will guide you through the basics and the extras for 21 gatherings and give you a special place to record memories, notes about what worked, and ideas for next time. May this inspire you and give you more confidence and motivation to gather often with old and new friends.

THE REASON TO GATHER

WHEN   WHERE

{ setting the tone }

MOOD   INSPIRATION

_____   _____
_____   _____
_____

COLOR PALETTE

{ menu }   # { guest list }

{ decor }

_____
_____
_____
_____
_____

{ tablescape elements }

LINENS

_____
_____
_____
_____

CENTERPIECE

_____
_____
_____
_____

PLACE SETTINGS

_____
_____
_____
_____

SPECIAL TOUCHES

_____
_____
_____
_____

{ activity }

_____
_____
_____
_____
_____

TO-DO LIST

SHOPPING LIST

☞ *Tip:* *Taper candles are a great staple to keep on hand. They add instant height, and when lit, they add that soft glow that creates a cozy, warm mood we are all drawn to.*

{ memorable moments }

{ remember for next time }

{ notes }

{ notes }

THE REASON TO GATHER

WHEN

WHERE

{ setting the tone }

MOOD

INSPIRATION

COLOR PALETTE

{ menu }

{ guest list }

{ decor }

_____
_____
_____
_____
_____

{ tablescape elements }

LINENS

_____
_____
_____
_____

CENTERPIECE

_____
_____
_____
_____

PLACE SETTINGS

_____
_____
_____
_____

SPECIAL TOUCHES

_____
_____
_____
_____

{ activity }

_____
_____
_____
_____

TO-DO LIST

SHOPPING LIST

"Dining with one's friends and beloved family is certainly one of life's primal and most innocent delights. One that is both soul-satisfying and eternal."
— Julia Child

{ memorable moments }

_____
_____
_____
_____
_____
_____
_____
_____
_____
_____
_____

{ remember for next time }

_____
_____
_____
_____
_____
_____
_____
_____
_____
_____
_____
_____

{ notes }

{ notes }

THE REASON TO GATHER

_____

WHEN   WHERE

{ setting the tone }

MOOD   INSPIRATION

_____   _____
_____   _____
_____   _____

COLOR PALETTE

_____ _____ _____

{ menu }   ## { guest list }

_____   _____
_____   _____
_____   _____
_____   _____
_____   _____
_____   _____
_____   _____
_____   _____

{ decor }

{ tablescape elements }

LINENS

CENTERPIECE

PLACE SETTINGS

SPECIAL TOUCHES

{ activity }

TO-DO LIST

_____

_____

_____

_____

_____

_____

_____

_____

_____

_____

_____

_____

_____

_____

_____

_____

_____

SHOPPING LIST

_____

_____

_____

_____

_____

_____

_____

_____

_____

_____

_____

_____

_____

_____

_____

_____

_____

☛ **_Tip:_** _Always check the care label on linens. It's helpful to be able to throw the tablecloth and cloth napkins and even placemats in the washing machine when you're finished with a gathering._

{ memorable moments }

{ remember for next time }

{ notes }

{ notes }

_____

THE REASON TO GATHER

_____   _____

WHEN   WHERE

{ setting the tone }

MOOD   INSPIRATION

_____   _____
_____   _____
_____   _____

COLOR PALETTE

_____   _____

{ menu }   ## *{ guest list }*

_____   _____
_____   _____
_____   _____
_____   _____
_____   _____
_____   _____
_____   _____
_____   _____
_____   _____
_____   _____

{ decor }

_____
_____
_____
_____
_____

{ tablescape elements }

LINENS

_____
_____
_____

CENTERPIECE

_____
_____
_____

PLACE SETTINGS

_____
_____
_____

SPECIAL TOUCHES

_____
_____
_____

{ activity }

_____
_____
_____
_____
_____

TO-DO LIST

_____
_____
_____
_____
_____
_____
_____
_____
_____
_____
_____
_____
_____
_____
_____
_____
_____
_____
_____

SHOPPING LIST

_____
_____
_____
_____
_____
_____
_____
_____
_____
_____
_____
_____
_____
_____
_____
_____
_____
_____

{ _"The fondest memories are made when gathered around the table."_
— _unknown_ }

{ memorable moments }

{ remember for next time }

{ notes }

{ notes }

_____

THE REASON TO GATHER

_____   _____
WHEN   WHERE

{ setting the tone }

MOOD   INSPIRATION

_____   _____
_____   _____
_____

COLOR PALETTE

_____

{ menu }   ## { guest list }

_____   _____
_____   _____
_____   _____
_____   _____
_____   _____
_____   _____
_____   _____
_____   _____
_____   _____

{ decor }

_____
_____
_____
_____
_____

{ tablescape elements }

LINENS

_____
_____
_____
_____

CENTERPIECE

_____
_____
_____
_____

PLACE SETTINGS

_____
_____
_____
_____

SPECIAL TOUCHES

_____
_____
_____
_____

{ activity }

_____
_____
_____
_____
_____

TO-DO LIST

SHOPPING LIST

Tip: *Layers add depth to your table. Try a ruffled tablecloth layered over another tablecloth. Experiment with a fluffy fur runner or cozy fleece blanket. Burlap coffee sacks add texture and layers. And sometimes a simple table runner on top of a rough-hewn table is all you need.*

{ memorable moments }

_____
_____
_____
_____
_____
_____
_____
_____
_____

{ remember for next time }

_____
_____
_____
_____
_____
_____
_____
_____
_____
_____

{ notes }

{ notes }

_____

THE REASON TO GATHER

_____   _____

WHEN   WHERE

{ setting the tone }

MOOD   INSPIRATION

_____   _____
_____   _____
_____   _____

COLOR PALETTE

_____   _____

{ menu }   *{ guest list }*

_____   _____
_____   _____
_____   _____
_____   _____
_____   _____
_____   _____
_____   _____
_____   _____

{ decor }

_____
_____
_____
_____
_____

{ tablescape elements }

LINENS

_____
_____
_____
_____

CENTERPIECE

_____
_____
_____
_____

PLACE SETTINGS

_____
_____
_____
_____

SPECIAL TOUCHES

_____
_____
_____
_____

{ activity }

_____
_____
_____
_____
_____

TO-DO LIST

SHOPPING LIST

"It is the sweet, simple things of life which are the real ones after all."
— *Laura Ingalls Wilder*

{ memorable moments }

{ remember for next time }

{ notes }

{ notes }

THE REASON TO GATHER

_____

WHEN   WHERE

{ setting the tone }

MOOD   INSPIRATION

_____   _____
_____   _____
_____   _____

COLOR PALETTE

_____

{ menu }   ## { guest list }

_____   _____
_____   _____
_____   _____
_____   _____
_____   _____
_____   _____
_____   _____
_____   _____

{ decor }

_____
_____
_____
_____

{ tablescape elements }

LINENS

_____
_____
_____

CENTERPIECE

_____
_____
_____

PLACE SETTINGS

_____
_____
_____

SPECIAL TOUCHES

_____
_____
_____

{ activity }

_____
_____
_____
_____

TO-DO LIST

_____
_____
_____
_____
_____
_____
_____
_____
_____
_____
_____
_____
_____
_____
_____
_____
_____
_____
_____
_____

SHOPPING LIST

_____
_____
_____
_____
_____
_____
_____
_____
_____
_____
_____
_____
_____
_____
_____
_____
_____
_____
_____
_____

☞ _**Tip:** Think about layers in your place settings. I always like to incorporate pieces that will help elevate each place setting on the table. Chargers stacked with plates, bowls instead of salad plates, name cards, and napkins wrapped with ribbons and ornaments all add layers to your place settings._

{ memorable moments }

{ remember for next time }

{ notes }

{ notes }

THE REASON TO GATHER

_____   _____
WHEN   WHERE

{ setting the tone }

MOOD   INSPIRATION

_____   _____
_____   _____
_____   _____

COLOR PALETTE

_____   _____

{ menu }   ## { guest list }

_____   _____
_____   _____
_____   _____
_____   _____
_____   _____
_____   _____
_____   _____
_____   _____

{ decor }

_____

_____

_____

_____

_____

{ tablescape elements }

LINENS

_____

_____

_____

_____

CENTERPIECE

_____

_____

_____

_____

PLACE SETTINGS

_____

_____

_____

_____

SPECIAL TOUCHES

_____

_____

_____

_____

{ activity }

_____

_____

_____

_____

TO-DO LIST

SHOPPING LIST

"When you have more than you need, build a longer table, not a higher fence."
— *unknown*

{ memorable moments }

{ remember for next time }

{ notes }

{ notes }

THE REASON TO GATHER

WHEN   WHERE

{ setting the tone }

MOOD   INSPIRATION

COLOR PALETTE

{ menu }   *{ guest list }*

{ decor }

_____
_____
_____
_____
_____

{ tablescape elements }

LINENS

_____
_____
_____
_____

CENTERPIECE

_____
_____
_____
_____

PLACE SETTINGS

_____
_____
_____
_____

SPECIAL TOUCHES

_____
_____
_____
_____

{ activity }

_____
_____
_____
_____
_____

TO-DO LIST

SHOPPING LIST

Tip: *Layers add interest to your centerpiece. Try an old barn board loaded up with candles or pumpkins, pieces of driftwood, a tray or a cutting board, cake stands with seasonal fruit arranged on top, or just some branches of greenery.*

{ memorable moments }

{ remember for next time }

{ notes }

{ notes }

THE REASON TO GATHER

WHEN

WHERE

{ setting the tone }

MOOD

INSPIRATION

COLOR PALETTE

{ menu }

{ guest list }

{ decor }

_____
_____
_____
_____
_____

{ tablescape elements }

LINENS

_____
_____
_____

CENTERPIECE

_____
_____
_____

PLACE SETTINGS

_____
_____
_____

SPECIAL TOUCHES

_____
_____
_____

{ activity }

_____
_____
_____
_____
_____

TO-DO LIST

SHOPPING LIST

"We do not remember days, we remember moments.
The richness of life lies in memories we have forgotten."
— Cesare Pavese

{ memorable moments }

{ remember for next time }

{ notes }

{ notes }

THE REASON TO GATHER

WHEN

WHERE

{ setting the tone }

MOOD

INSPIRATION

COLOR PALETTE

{ menu }

{ guest list }

{ decor }

_____
_____
_____
_____
_____

{ tablescape elements }

LINENS

_____
_____
_____
_____

CENTERPIECE

_____
_____
_____
_____

PLACE SETTINGS

_____
_____
_____
_____

SPECIAL TOUCHES

_____
_____
_____
_____

{ activity }

_____
_____
_____
_____

TO-DO LIST

SHOPPING LIST

Tip: The overall height and silhouette of your tablescape has great impact on the impression and mood of the presentation. Try adding height and interest with cake stands, candlesticks, vases, trays, buckets, a collection of vintage bottles, stacked books, tree branches arranged in vases that reach for the ceiling, and so on.

{ memorable moments }

{ remember for next time }

{ notes }

{ *notes* }

THE REASON TO GATHER

_____

WHEN   WHERE

_____

{ setting the tone }

MOOD   INSPIRATION

_____   _____
_____   _____
_____   _____

COLOR PALETTE

_____   _____

{ menu }   ### { guest list }

_____   _____
_____   _____
_____   _____
_____   _____
_____   _____
_____   _____
_____   _____
_____   _____

{ decor }

_____

_____

_____

_____

_____

{ tablescape elements }

LINENS

_____

_____

_____

_____

CENTERPIECE

_____

_____

_____

_____

PLACE SETTINGS

_____

_____

_____

SPECIAL TOUCHES

_____

_____

_____

{ activity }

_____

_____

_____

_____

TO-DO LIST

SHOPPING LIST

{ memorable moments }

_____
_____
_____
_____
_____
_____
_____

{ remember for next time }

_____
_____
_____
_____
_____
_____
_____
_____
_____
_____

{ notes }

{ notes }

THE REASON TO GATHER

WHEN

WHERE

{ setting the tone }

MOOD

INSPIRATION

COLOR PALETTE

{ menu }

{ guest list }

{ decor }

_____
_____
_____
_____
_____

{ tablescape elements }

LINENS

_____
_____
_____
_____

CENTERPIECE

_____
_____
_____
_____

PLACE SETTINGS

_____
_____
_____
_____

SPECIAL TOUCHES

_____
_____
_____
_____

{ activity }

_____
_____
_____
_____
_____

TO-DO LIST

_____
_____
_____
_____
_____
_____
_____
_____
_____
_____
_____
_____
_____
_____
_____
_____
_____
_____
_____
_____

SHOPPING LIST

_____
_____
_____
_____
_____
_____
_____
_____
_____
_____
_____
_____
_____
_____
_____
_____
_____
_____
_____
_____

☛ *Tip:* *When adding height to your centerpiece, a good rule of thumb is to avoid adding anything so high that your guests can't see over it. I've been known to break this rule from time to time, which usually results in my husband removing the item from the table as we sit down to eat.*

{ memorable moments }

_____

_____

_____

_____

_____

_____

_____

_____

_____

{ remember for next time }

_____

_____

_____

_____

_____

_____

_____

_____

_____

_____

_____

{ notes }

{ notes }

THE REASON TO GATHER

WHEN

WHERE

{ setting the tone }

MOOD

INSPIRATION

COLOR PALETTE

{ menu }

{ guest list }

{ decor }

_____

_____

_____

_____

_____

{ tablescape elements }

LINENS

_____

_____

_____

_____

CENTERPIECE

_____

_____

_____

_____

PLACE SETTINGS

_____

_____

_____

_____

SPECIAL TOUCHES

_____

_____

_____

_____

{ activity }

_____

_____

_____

_____

_____

TO-DO LIST

SHOPPING LIST

"Cooking is one of the great gifts you can give to those you love."
— *Ina Garten*

{ memorable moments }

{ remember for next time }

{ notes }

{ notes }

THE REASON TO GATHER

WHEN

WHERE

{ setting the tone }

MOOD

INSPIRATION

COLOR PALETTE

{ menu }

{ guest list }

{ decor }

_____
_____
_____
_____
_____

{ tablescape elements }

LINENS

_____
_____
_____
_____

CENTERPIECE

_____
_____
_____
_____

PLACE SETTINGS

_____
_____
_____
_____

SPECIAL TOUCHES

_____
_____
_____
_____

{ activity }

_____
_____
_____
_____
_____

TO-DO LIST

_____

_____

_____

_____

_____

_____

_____

_____

_____

_____

_____

_____

_____

_____

_____

_____

_____

_____

_____

_____

SHOPPING LIST

_____

_____

_____

_____

_____

_____

_____

_____

_____

_____

_____

_____

_____

_____

_____

_____

_____

_____

_____

_____

☛ **Tip:** *Incorporating texture is a great way to involve the senses when creating a table. It instantly adds warmth that makes guests feel welcome.*

{ memorable moments }

_____
_____
_____
_____
_____
_____
_____
_____
_____

{ remember for next time }

_____
_____
_____
_____
_____
_____
_____
_____
_____
_____
_____

{ notes }

{ notes }

THE REASON TO GATHER

WHEN   WHERE

{ setting the tone }

MOOD   INSPIRATION

_____   _____
_____   _____
_____   _____

COLOR PALETTE

_____   _____   _____

{ menu }   ## { guest list }

{ decor }

_____
_____
_____
_____
_____

{ tablescape elements }

LINENS

_____
_____
_____
_____

CENTERPIECE

_____
_____
_____
_____

PLACE SETTINGS

_____
_____
_____
_____

SPECIAL TOUCHES

_____
_____
_____
_____

{ activity }

_____
_____
_____
_____
_____

TO-DO LIST

SHOPPING LIST

"People who love to eat are always the best people."
— *Julia Child*

{ memorable moments }

{ remember for next time }

{ notes }

{ notes }

THE REASON TO GATHER

WHEN

WHERE

{ setting the tone }

MOOD

INSPIRATION

COLOR PALETTE

{ menu }

{ guest list }

{ decor }

_____
_____
_____
_____
_____

{ tablescape elements }

LINENS

_____
_____
_____
_____

CENTERPIECE

_____
_____
_____
_____

PLACE SETTINGS

_____
_____
_____
_____

SPECIAL TOUCHES

_____
_____
_____
_____

{ activity }

_____
_____
_____
_____
_____

TO-DO LIST

SHOPPING LIST

☛ ***Tip:*** *Think seasonally when it comes to adding natural elements to your table. Try bare branches in winter, and go for a pop of green in springtime. Summer is the time for fresh flowers, and fall is all about the squash and pumpkins.*

{ memorable moments }

{ remember for next time }

{ notes }

{ notes }

THE REASON TO GATHER

WHEN

WHERE

{ setting the tone }

MOOD

INSPIRATION

COLOR PALETTE

{ menu }

{ guest list }

{ decor }

_____

_____

_____

_____

_____

{ tablescape elements }

LINENS

_____

_____

_____

_____

CENTERPIECE

_____

_____

_____

_____

PLACE SETTINGS

_____

_____

_____

_____

SPECIAL TOUCHES

_____

_____

_____

_____

{ activity }

_____

_____

_____

_____

_____

TO-DO LIST

SHOPPING LIST

"If you want to bring happiness to the whole world, go home and love your family."
— *Mother Teresa*

{ memorable moments }

{ remember for next time }

{ *notes* }

{ notes }

THE REASON TO GATHER

WHEN   WHERE

{ setting the tone }

MOOD   INSPIRATION

COLOR PALETTE

{ menu }   *{ guest list }*

{ decor }

_____

_____

_____

_____

{ tablescape elements }

LINENS

_____

_____

_____

_____

CENTERPIECE

_____

_____

_____

_____

PLACE SETTINGS

_____

_____

_____

_____

SPECIAL TOUCHES

_____

_____

_____

_____

{ activity }

_____

_____

_____

_____

_____

TO-DO LIST

SHOPPING LIST

☞ *Tip: Mixing and matching instantly gives you a relaxed, eclectic look. It creates a one-of-a-kind feel that adds instant charm to your table.*

{ memorable moments }

{ remember for next time }

{ notes }

{ notes }

THE REASON TO GATHER

WHEN   WHERE

{ setting the tone }

MOOD   INSPIRATION

COLOR PALETTE

{ menu }   *{ guest list }*

{ decor }

_____
_____
_____
_____

{ tablescape elements }

LINENS

_____
_____
_____

CENTERPIECE

_____
_____
_____

PLACE SETTINGS

_____
_____
_____

SPECIAL TOUCHES

_____
_____
_____

{ activity }

_____
_____
_____
_____

TO-DO LIST

_____
_____
_____
_____
_____
_____
_____
_____
_____
_____
_____
_____
_____
_____
_____
_____
_____
_____

SHOPPING LIST

_____
_____
_____
_____
_____
_____
_____
_____
_____
_____
_____
_____
_____
_____
_____
_____
_____
_____

{ *"Food is not about impressing people. It's about making them feel comfortable."*
— *Ina Garten* }

{ memorable moments }

{ remember for next time }

{ notes }

{ notes }

THE REASON TO GATHER

WHEN   WHERE

{ setting the tone }

MOOD   INSPIRATION

_____   _____
_____   _____
_____   _____

COLOR PALETTE

_____   _____

{ menu }   ## { guest list }

_____   _____
_____   _____
_____   _____
_____   _____
_____   _____
_____   _____
_____   _____
_____   _____

{ decor }

_____

_____

_____

_____

{ tablescape elements }

LINENS

_____

_____

_____

CENTERPIECE

_____

_____

_____

PLACE SETTINGS

_____

_____

_____

SPECIAL TOUCHES

_____

_____

_____

{ activity }

_____

_____

_____

_____

TO-DO LIST

_____
_____
_____
_____
_____
_____
_____
_____
_____
_____
_____
_____
_____
_____
_____
_____
_____
_____
_____

SHOPPING LIST

_____
_____
_____
_____
_____
_____
_____
_____
_____
_____
_____
_____
_____
_____
_____
_____
_____
_____
_____

☛ *Tip: Your look will be richer with the addition of antiques. The sense of history and story they bring to the table adds instant interest. Some favorite go-to items include candlesticks, salt and pepper shakers, silverware, trays, tiny bowls, and teapots.*

{ memorable moments }

{ remember for next time }

{ notes }

{ notes }

 **APPETIZERS**

Buffalo Chicken Dip

PREP TIME: 10 MINUTES | YIELDS: 5 SERVINGS

This delicious offering always tops my short list when we are invited to someone's house. I love how easily this recipe comes together. It combines all the familiar flavors of buffalo wings—without the mess of trying to eat them—transformed into a warm and bubbly dip!

INGREDIENTS

1½ cups chicken, cooked and shredded

1 (8 oz.) package cream cheese, softened

¾ cup buffalo sauce
(we like Frank's RedHot Buffalo Wings Sauce)

½ cup sharp cheddar cheese, shredded

☛ *Tip: I like to use a rotisserie chicken from the grocery store to save time on cooking the chicken.*

DIRECTIONS

Preheat the oven to 375°. In a large bowl, combine the chicken, cream cheese, buffalo sauce, and cheddar cheese. Transfer the mixture to an 8 x 8-inch baking dish and bake for 20 minutes or until it's bubbly. Top with scallions (optional) and serve warm with tortilla chips, sliced bread, or celery sticks.

Peach & Blue Cheese Crostini

PREP TIME: 15 MINUTES | **YIELDS:** 10 SERVINGS

When I want to put in a little more effort, this elegant appetizer is the perfect blend of sweet and tangy flavors. It's best when fresh peaches are in season (I would not recommend canned), or you can use apple or pear slices instead of peaches. A fancy treat for an adults' night in.

INGREDIENTS

1 baguette, cut into ½-inch slices
2 T. olive oil
1 or 2 peaches, pitted and sliced into thin wedges

8 oz. blue cheese
2 or 3 T. honey

DIRECTIONS

Preheat the oven to 400°. Arrange the baguette slices on a cookie sheet, and lightly brush the olive oil over the slices. Bake for 7 minutes or until the slices are lightly toasted. Place 1 or 2 peach slices on each piece of bread. Sprinkle blue cheese crumbles on the peach slices, and place back in the oven for 5 to 7 minutes or until the cheese is melted. Remove from the oven and transfer to a serving platter. Drizzle with honey and serve warm.

Party Pleasing Dip

PREP TIME: 10 MINUTES | YIELDS: 12-14 SERVINGS

Perfect for serving a crowd! This yields a large portion, which is great when your guest list is long or when you host a "come one, come all" event and aren't sure how many people will attend. This is a tasty offering for any gathering, and it's my go-to for birthday parties, barbecues, Super Bowl parties, or taco night!

INGREDIENTS

6 roma tomatoes, diced

1 red pepper, diced

1 green pepper, diced

2 jalapeño peppers, diced

½ purple onion, diced

1 (15 oz.) can corn, drained

1 (15 oz.) can black beans, drained and rinsed

1 large avocado, peeled, pitted, and diced

½ bunch cilantro, about 1 cup chopped

⅓ cup fresh lime juice (juice of 2 limes)

1 T. chili powder

1 T. garlic powder

1 T. onion powder

salt and pepper to taste

2 to 3 T. garlic, minced

1 T. cumin

DIRECTIONS

In a large mixing bowl, combine the diced tomatoes, peppers, onion, corn, black beans, avocado, and cilantro. Stir in the lime juice, garlic, and dried seasonings, and mix well. Serve with your favorite tortilla chips! We like to mix yellow and blue corn tortilla chips for an extra-colorful presentation of this tasty appetizer!

Easy Olive Oil & Pesto Dip

PREP TIME: 5 MINUTES | YIELDS: 6 SERVINGS

We love bread! I mean, *love* bread. This easy appetizer comes together in minutes and offers all the elegance of dining at a fancy Italian restaurant!

INGREDIENTS

2 T. grated Parmesan cheese

1 T. basil, dried

1 T. parsley, dried

1 tsp. oregano, dried

½ tsp. crushed red pepper

1 tsp. black pepper

½ tsp. salt

1 loaf French bread, sliced and cubed

2 cups olive oil

DIRECTIONS

Combine the cheese, herbs, and spices in a small bowl. In a dipping bowl, combine the olive oil with either those mixed dry ingredients or ½ of a small jar of pesto. Place the dipping bowl in the center of a large serving tray and arrange the bread cubes all around.

Brussels Sprouts Aioli

PREP TIME: 15 MINUTES | YIELDS: 4-5 SERVINGS

Brussels sprouts can have a bad reputation. But I can attest that once you've prepared them like this, you will not only want them more often, you'll also want them no other way. The secret is the flavor that emerges from the oven roasting combined with the creamy garlic aioli! Do not be intimidated by the aioli. I assure you, when these pantry staple ingredients are mixed together just right, you'll be praising this vegetable in no time.

INGREDIENTS

2 T. olive oil
1 lb. brussels sprouts, halved
1 tsp. garlic powder
½ tsp. salt
pepper to taste

For the Aioli:
¼ cup mayonnaise
4 T. lemon juice
2 T. olive oil
½ tsp. garlic powder
½ tsp. salt

DIRECTIONS

Preheat the oven to 450°. Drizzle the olive oil on a cookie sheet. Spread the brussels sprouts on the cookie sheet and sprinkle with the garlic powder, salt, and pepper. Toss to coat them evenly. Bake for 20 minutes or until crispy.

While the brussels sprouts are baking, combine all the ingredients for the aioli in a small bowl and whisk until smooth. Once the sprouts are done roasting, pour the aioli mixture on top and toss until they are evenly coated. Serve warm.

Blueberry and Walnut Arugula Salad

PREP TIME: 5 MINUTES | YIELDS: 4 SERVINGS

These four simple ingredients tossed together make one very flavorful salad! Sometimes underrated, a simple salad can be transformed into an elegant side dish with the right flavor combination. The best part of this salad is that there are no veggies to chop. Just rinse the ingredients and fill your favorite salad bowl for a beautiful presentation.

INGREDIENTS

6 cups arugula

1 cup blueberries

⅔ cup walnuts

½ cup feta cheese

For the dressing:

¼ cup lemon juice, freshly squeezed

½ cup olive oil

1 tsp. granulated sugar

1 tsp. kosher salt

½ tsp. fresh ground pepper

DIRECTIONS

Combine the arugula, blueberries, walnuts, and feta in a large serving bowl. Toss with the dressing just before serving so the arugula does not wilt.

Snappy Pasta Salad

PREP TIME: 20 MINUTES | YIELDS: 8-10 SERVINGS

My mom used to make this all the time when I was growing up. In high school I enjoyed endless bowls of this pasta salad as afternoon snacks, weekend lunches, and a staple at gatherings. My sisters and I used to fight over who would get the last bowl. The ingredients are simple, but they will keep your guests coming back for more!

INGREDIENTS

1 (12 oz.) box tricolor rotini pasta

1 cucumber, peeled and chopped

1 pint of cherry tomatoes, halved

½ green pepper, chopped

½ red pepper, chopped

⅓ cup red onion, diced

1 (2.25 oz.) can sliced black olives

½ cup feta cheese

1 (12 fl. oz.) bottle of your favorite Italian salad dressing

DIRECTIONS

Cook the pasta according to the instructions on the box. When the pasta is done, drain the noodles and run cold water over them. In a large bowl, combine the cooked pasta with the rest of the ingredients and ¾ of the salad dressing. You can serve this salad right away, but it's best when refrigerated for 1 or 2 hours before serving. Pour the remaining ¼ of the salad dressing over the pasta salad just before serving and toss gently.

Must-Have Mashed Potatoes

PREP TIME: 15 MINUTES | YIELDS: 4-5 SERVINGS

We probably have mashed potatoes in our house once a week! They are my son's favorite, so I've gotten pretty good at making these quickly. No longer reserved just for holidays, these mouthwatering mashed potatoes are the perfect side to go with almost any meal. To cut back on prep time, I wash the potatoes but leave the skin on, and I cut the potatoes into quarters before boiling.

INGREDIENTS

1.5 lbs. baby gold potatoes
½ cup butter
½ cup sour cream

⅓ cup heavy cream
kosher salt and freshly ground pepper to taste

DIRECTIONS

Boil the potatoes until cooked. Drain them in a colander. Leave the potatoes in the colander and return the pot to the stove. Melt the butter in the pot on low heat. Then turn the burner off and add the potatoes back into the pot. Mash the potatoes to your desired consistency (we like ours a little lumpy with the skin on). Stir in the sour cream and heavy cream, and season generously with kosher salt and freshly ground pepper to taste. Serve immediately.

Slow-Cooker Beef Stew

PREP TIME: 35 MINUTES | YIELDS: 8-10 SERVINGS

This hearty beef stew is our favorite comfort food during the fall and winter months. The best part about this recipe is not how tender it makes the beef (although that's amazing!) but how the slow-cooking process allows you to prepare everything in advance, saving you time in the kitchen before guests arrive. It gives the impression that you've been working hard in the kitchen all day, but really, the slow cooker does all the work. It's the perfect go-to for anyone who wants to entertain but is intimidated by preparing an elaborate meal.

INGREDIENTS

1½ lbs. boneless beef chuck roast (1-inch cubes)

1 (13.5 fl. oz.) can cream of mushroom soup

3 medium potatoes, peeled and cubed

4 to 6 medium carrots, peeled and chopped

1 medium onion, chopped

1 or 2 celery ribs, chopped

2 cups beef broth

1 garlic clove, minced

1 or 2 dried bay leaves

1 or 2 sprigs fresh thyme

1 tsp. oregano

2 tsp. onion powder

1 tsp. salt

½ tsp. pepper

2 cups frozen peas

DIRECTIONS

Place the beef, potatoes, carrots, garlic, onion, celery, beef broth, and all seasonings in a 5-to 6-quart slow cooker. Cover and cook on low for 5 to 7 hours. Then add the frozen peas and cream of mushroom soup. Stir and cook for 1 more hour. Serve with your favorite crusty loaf of bread.

Barbecue Chicken Nachos

PREP TIME: 15 MINUTES | **YIELDS:** 6-8 SERVINGS *(party size)*

Nachos are kind of our thing. Over the years, in the quest to recreate our favorite restaurant nachos, we have come up with this crowd pleaser. I have it listed as a meal because it is so easy to throw together and serve as a main dish. You could easily serve this as an appetizer for a larger crowd.

INGREDIENTS

2 (11 oz.) bags of salted tortilla chips

4 to 6 T. garlic, freshly minced

1 green pepper, chopped

2 or 3 fresh jalapeños, sliced

1 medium onion, chopped

2 to 3 cups sharp cheddar cheese, shredded

1 or 2 cooked chicken breasts, cooked and shredded

Barbecue sauce of choice *(we like Sweet Baby Ray's)*

1 bunch cilantro, freshly chopped

☛ ***Tip:*** *The crunchier the chips, the better. You do not want thin tortilla chips for this because they become too soggy and flimsy once baked.*

DIRECTIONS

Move the oven rack to the top shelf and set the oven to broil at 500°. Keep the oven door slightly cracked when broiling. Line the cookie sheet with one even layer of tortilla chips. Sprinkle the chips with half the garlic, green pepper, jalapeño, and onion. Spread half the shredded cheese over the tortilla chips and vegetables so they are covered well. Top with half the chicken and drizzle barbecue sauce on top. Broil 6 to 8 minutes—just until the cheese has melted. Remove from the oven and assemble your second (top) layer of nachos, repeating all the steps. Return to the oven and broil 7 to 9 minutes, or until the cheese is melted, beginning to bubble, and browned around the edges. Remove from the oven and sprinkle with the cilantro. Serve with sour cream. Confession: We like to eat these nachos right off the cookie sheet!

 **MAIN DISHES**

No-Fail Barbecue Chicken

PREP TIME: 10 MINUTES | **YIELDS:** 6 SERVINGS

The key to achieving perfect barbecue chicken is slow-cooking it on the grill. This requires a labor of love, but once you've tasted this, you won't regret the time spent. We usually start the grilling process 1½ hours before we want to eat so we don't let our hungry tummies rush the process.

INGREDIENTS

2 to 3 lbs. chicken

For the dry rub*:

½ cup paprika

¼ cup kosher salt

¼ cup sugar

2 T. mustard powder

¼ cup chili powder

¼ cup ground cumin

2 T. ground black pepper

¼ cup granulated garlic

2 T. cayenne

*Place the dry rub ingredients in a large ziplock to toss the chicken.

For the barbecue sauce:

2 cups ketchup

¼ cup cider vinegar

¼ cup Worcestershire sauce

¼ cup brown sugar, firmly packed

2 T. molasses

3 T. prepared yellow mustard

2 T. dry rub *(see recipe)*

½ tsp. black pepper

Hot sauce to taste

(we like Frank's RedHot Buffalo Wings Sauce)

☛ *Tip: Toss the chicken in the dry rub the day before to allow the chicken to marinate.*

DIRECTIONS

Simmer the sauce ingredients in a saucepan for 10 to 15 minutes to thicken.

Grill the chicken with the dry rub (but no sauce) on low heat for 30 to 35 minutes, turning halfway through. Once the chicken is golden, about ½ of the way done, turn the grill up to medium-high heat and cook for 15 minutes, brushing the sauce on one side at a time. Flip the chicken often and continue brushing on the sauce, generously coating the chicken on both sides. Use a meat thermometer to make sure the chicken is cooked all the way (about 165°). Transfer the chicken to a platter and cover it with foil for 5 to 10 minutes before serving.

Baked Salmon

PREP TIME: 10 MINUTES | YIELDS: 6 SERVINGS

I love to serve salmon when we have company. People don't often make it for themselves, so it feels like a treat. This easy salmon recipe is an elegant option and makes any occasion special.

INGREDIENTS

1½ to 2 lbs. fresh salmon

2 to 3 T. olive oil

2 T. Cajun or creole seasoning

½ tsp. salt

¼ tsp. pepper

DIRECTIONS

Preheat the oven to 425°. Line a cookie sheet with foil (I use 2 sheets of foil per cookie sheet). Place the salmon on the cookie sheet, skin side down. Drizzle with the olive oil. Sprinkle the seasoning, salt, and pepper, and begin rubbing it over the salmon, spreading evenly. Add additional olive oil as needed if the seasoning appears too dry. Bake 25 minutes for thicker pieces (begin checking thin pieces at 16 minutes to avoid overcooking). Salmon is completely cooked when the center is light pink. Using a spatula, gently remove the salmon from the cookie sheet by separating it from the skin, leaving the skin behind.

Angel Cake Parfait

PREP TIME: 20 MINUTES | YIELDS: 10-12 SERVINGS

During their early childhood years, my kids started calling angel food cake simply angel cake. Even though the kids are older now, I still use the nickname because it makes me happy! This parfait offers a simple twist on a classic favorite and is heavenly for entertaining. I make these individual desserts in mason jars ahead of time so they're easy to transport outside when we are hosting backyard parties in the summer.

INGREDIENTS

2 packages Jell-O cheesecake instant pudding mix

4 cups milk (for pudding mix)

2 lbs. strawberries, hulled and quartered

¼ cup granulated sugar

1 pint heavy whipping cream

¼ cup confectioners' sugar

1 tsp. vanilla extract

1 angel food cake

(store-bought works just fine and saves you time in the kitchen)

DIRECTIONS

Prepare the pudding, following the instructions on the box.

In a large bowl, combine the strawberries and granulated sugar. Mix until the strawberries are coated with sugar, and leave them at room temperature about 15 minutes (until the strawberry juices extract), stirring occasionally. While the strawberries sit, prepare the whipped cream. Using an electric mixer on high speed, beat together the heavy whipping cream, confectioners' sugar, and vanilla extract until soft peaks form.

To assemble the dessert, create layers using torn-apart angel cake, a large spoonful of cheesecake pudding, 2 tablespoons strawberries, and then a large spoonful of whipped cream. Repeat until you have 3 layers, finishing with the whipped cream on top. Serve immediately or cover with plastic wrap and refrigerate until serving. *Fills 6 1-quart mason jars or 1 trifle dish.*

Grilled Peaches & Pound Cake

PREP TIME: 15 MINUTES | YIELDS: 6 SERVINGS

This summertime dessert whips up in no time and is our favorite to share with friends. The secret is in grilling the pound cake. Warm, crisp grilled pound cake and peaches that have caramelized on the grill partner perfectly with cold ice cream on hot summer nights. Here's my hosting hack: Eliminate all baking and buy a fresh pound cake from your grocery store.

INGREDIENTS

5 or 6 ripe peaches, halved and pitted
1 T. butter, melted
¼ cup brown sugar

1 tsp. cinnamon
1 pound cake, sliced in 1-inch slices
butter pecan ice cream

DIRECTIONS

Preheat the grill or cast-iron skillet to medium heat. Lightly brush the peaches with melted butter. Place the peaches on the grill or pan with the cut side down and cook for 2 to 4 minutes. Flip the peaches over, sprinkle with brown sugar and cinnamon, and grill for another 2 to 3 minutes, or until the sugar mixture begins to caramelize.

Grill the pound cake slices for 2 minutes on each side. Remove the pound cake and peaches from grill and slice the peaches (this gets a little messy, but they are so yummy!). Assemble the dessert with 1 slice of pound cake, 2 spoons of grilled peaches, and 1 scoop of ice cream. Vanilla ice cream is nice, but we've found that butter pecan ice cream takes this dessert to the next level.

Caramel Chocolate Trifle

PREP TIME: 15 MINUTES | **YIELDS:** 12-14 SERVINGS *(party size)*

Picture this: decadent layers of moist chocolate cake paired with layers of gooey caramel and light, fluffy homemade whipped cream, topped with the crumbled-up sweetness of a toffee bar. This dessert will be your hosting friend because it tastes even better when you make it the day before company comes.

INGREDIENTS

1 pint heavy whipping cream

¼ cup confectioners' sugar

1 tsp. vanilla extract

1 chocolate cake, baked and cooled

1 (14 oz.) can sweetened condensed milk

1½ cup caramel sauce

⅓ cup Heath bar crumbles

DIRECTIONS

Using an electric mixer on high speed, beat together the heavy whipping cream, sugar, and vanilla extract until soft peaks form.

Cut the cake into 1-inch cubes. Place half on the bottom of your trifle dish. Pour half of the sweetened condensed milk across the top and then half of the caramel sauce. Sprinkle with half of the Heath bar pieces and finish with half of the whipped cream. Repeat the cake, milk, caramel, Heath bar crumbles, and whipped cream layer. Sprinkle the top with more Heath bar pieces. Let the trifle sit 4 to 6 hours or overnight in the fridge.

Apple Pie Cheesecake Bars

PREP TIME: 20 MINUTES | YIELDS: 12 SERVINGS

Apple picking is a favorite autumn tradition here in New England. And my husband loves making fresh apple pie. Bless him! So we paired our favorite fall dessert with creamy cheesecake for the ultimate dessert. You can make this with a graham cracker crust or, for a fun twist, the gingersnap crust I love.

INGREDIENTS

30 gingersnap cookies

½ cup and 3 T. sugar

½ cup (1 stick) butter, softened

2 (8 oz.) packages cream cheese

½ cup sour cream

1 egg

½ cup confectioners' sugar

5 green apples, peeled, cored, and diced

¼ cup apple juice

1 T. cornstarch

1 T. cinnamon

DIRECTIONS

Preheat the oven to 350°. Break up the cookies into a food processor and pulse with 3 tablespoons of the sugar until combined. Transfer to a bowl, combine with 5 tablespoons of butter, and mix well. Line an 8 x 8-inch baking dish with foil, grease it, and then press the cookie mixture into the bottom of pan. Beat the cream cheese, sour cream, egg, and confectioners' sugar until smooth, and spread it over the crust in pan. Bake for 40 minutes.

Melt the remaining butter in a large skillet over medium heat. Add the apple pieces and sauté 5 minutes. In a small bowl, blend the apple juice and cornstarch. Add the remaining sugar, the cinnamon, and the cornstarch mixture to the skillet and cook until it's bubbly and thick.

When the cheesecake bars are done, pour the apple mixture on top and spread evenly. Bake 5 more minutes. Refrigerate until chilled (at least 1 hour) and cut into bars. Garnish with confectioners' sugar and cinnamon sprinkled on top just before serving.

MY GO-TO RECIPES

Recipe:

PREP TIME: SERVINGS:

INGREDIENTS   DIRECTIONS

Recipe:

PREP TIME: SERVINGS:

INGREDIENTS   DIRECTIONS

Recipe:

PREP TIME: **SERVINGS:**

INGREDIENTS

DIRECTIONS

Recipe:

PREP TIME: **SERVINGS:**

INGREDIENTS

DIRECTIONS

Recipe:

PREP TIME:　　　　**SERVINGS:**

INGREDIENTS　　　　　　　　**DIRECTIONS**

Recipe:

PREP TIME:　　　　**SERVINGS:**

INGREDIENTS　　　　　　　　**DIRECTIONS**

Recipe:

PREP TIME: SERVINGS:

INGREDIENTS   **DIRECTIONS**

Recipe:

PREP TIME: SERVINGS:

INGREDIENTS   **DIRECTIONS**

Recipe:

PREP TIME: **SERVINGS:**

INGREDIENTS

DIRECTIONS

Recipe:

PREP TIME: **SERVINGS:**

INGREDIENTS

DIRECTIONS

Recipe:

PREP TIME: SERVINGS:

INGREDIENTS   DIRECTIONS

Recipe:

PREP TIME: SERVINGS:

INGREDIENTS   DIRECTIONS

Recipe:

PREP TIME: **SERVINGS:**

INGREDIENTS   **DIRECTIONS**

Recipe:

PREP TIME: **SERVINGS:**

INGREDIENTS   **DIRECTIONS**

Recipe:

PREP TIME: SERVINGS:

INGREDIENTS   DIRECTIONS

Recipe:

PREP TIME: SERVINGS:

INGREDIENTS   DIRECTIONS

MY HOSTESS GIFT TO YOU

{ *Whoever refreshes others will be refreshed.*
PROVERBS 11:25 }

Refresh your spirit. Give yourself the joy of discovery by paying attention to details and all that pleases your senses throughout the day. You will be surprised how ideas and interesting visual delights can inspire your heart for the next gathering. This becomes one amazing adventure in observation and wonder. The special touches you use in your home and your tablescape will be received with appreciation and affection. All you need to do now is sit at the table with a glad and sincere heart.

Take a deep breath. Don't strive for perfection. Be sure to stay true to yourself. Your guests are coming to fellowship with you. So enjoy the planning, preparing, and serving as you anticipate the gifts to come: laughter, conversations about life, platters of food passed with love, and the exchange of ideas and hopes. Your spirit is ready to treasure the people you welcome to your table and into your life.

Be refreshed, my friend. Be blessed.

A BLESSING

God, grant me a spirit of wonder as I prepare to serve love and hospitality through special touches and a welcoming home. Refresh me and those who gather around the table. May we use these times to honor the gifts we see unfolding in each other and through our fellowship.

Give us our daily bread so we are nourished, strengthened, and inspired to share seasons of meaning. May I expand my heart and my sense of home and family. Bless all who celebrate life together and who break bread as friends, family, and community.

Amen.